The Stay at Home Gratitude Journal:

5 Minute Inspirational Prompts, Questions and Quotes for Overcoming Negativity

Dreamstorm Publications

Your Personal Space:

Vision board or inspirational photos. Your choice.

Your Personal Space:

Vision board or inspirational photos. Your choice.

Day 1 __/__/__

"Life is too short to spend in negativity. So I have made a conscious effort to not be where I don't want to be."
– Hugh Dillon

Today, I am grateful for…

People say, "Every cloud has a silver lining." What does this phrase mean to you?

Day 2 __/__/__

"A positive attitude may not solve every problem
but it makes solving any problem a more pleasant experience."
– Grant Fairley

Today, I am grateful for…

What is the nicest thing you have ever done for yourself?

Day 3 __/__/__

"All negativity is an illusion created
by the limited mind to protect and defend itself."
– Ambika Wauters

Today, I am grateful for…

What negative beliefs do you hold about yourself?

Day 4 __/__/__

"All the negativity that was once around me
has turned into all this positivity."
– Brian Banks

Today, I am grateful for…

What habit do you need to stop?

Day 5 __/__/__

"All things are difficult before they are easy."
– Thomas Fuller

Today, I am grateful for…

What parts of your life would you like to work on improving?

Day 6 __/__/__

"Always think extra hard before crossing over to a bad side, if you were weak enough to cross over, you may not be strong enough to cross back!" – Victoria Addino

Today, I am grateful for…

Why do you think self-worth is important?

Day 7 __/__/__

"An entire sea of water can't sink a ship unless it gets inside the ship. Similarly, the negativity of the world can't put you down unless you allow it to get inside you." – Goi Nasu

Today, I am grateful for…

How would your life change if you were confident?

Day 8 __/__/__

"As soon as you replace negative thoughts with positive ones, you will start to get positive results."
– Wilie Nelson

Today, I am grateful for…

What parts of your life are you happy with?

Day 9 __/__/__

"Be thankful for everything that happens in your life;
it's all an experience."
– Roy T. Bennet

Today, I am grateful for…

When do you feel most confident?

Day 10 __/__/__

"Being miserable is a habit; being happy is a habit,
and the choice is yours."
– Tom Hopkins

Today, I am grateful for…

What is your favorite thing to do to treat yourself?

Day 11 __/__/__

"Determination Over Negativity is a belief that anything is possible no matter who you are or where you come from."
– Donovan Mitchell

Today, I am grateful for…

What are things that you need to stop doing that are making you unhappy?

Day 12 __/__/__

"Do not allow negative people to turn you into one of them."
– Anonymous

Today, I am grateful for…

I am happiest when…

Day 13 __/__/__

"Don't let negative and toxic people rent space in your head.
Raise the rent and kick them out."
– Robert Tew

Today, I am grateful for…

What do you think your biggest weakness is? How can you work on improving this?

Day 14 _/_/_

"Don't spend energy on worries or negative thoughts."
– Bruce Lee

Today, I am grateful for…

Think of something that has bothered you lately. Do you think you will still care about it in a month? Or in a year? Why or why not?

Day 15 __/__/__

"Each problem has hidden in it an opportunity so powerful that it literally dwarfs the problem. The greatest success stories were created by people who recognized a problem and turned it into an opportunity." – Joseph Sugarman

Today, I am grateful for…

People say, "Laughter is the best medicine." What is something that always makes you laugh? Does it make you feel better when you are upset?

Day 16 __/__/__

"Every day you must unlearn the ways that hold you back. You must rid yourself of negativity, so you can learn to fly."
– Leon Brown

Today, I am grateful for…

What is one healthy habit you could maintain each day that would have a positive effect on your life?

Day 17 __/__/__

"Experiencing sadness and anger can make you feel more creative, and by being creative, you can get beyond your pain or negativity." – Yoko Ono

Today, I am grateful for…

Think of something that scares you. Then, consider a reason you don't need to be scared of it and write about your thoughts.

Day 18 __/__/__

"Fall seven times and stand up eight."
– Japanese Proverb

Today, I am grateful for…

Write about a time when you used positive thinking to reframe a negative situation.

Day 19 __/__/__

"Guard your heart above all else,
for it determines the course of your life."
– Proverbs 4:23 (NLT)

Today, I am grateful for…

Think of one nice thing you can do for a stranger today. Then, write about what you will do.

Day 20 __/__/__

"Habits are patterned repetitions. Dispose of repeating the negative which is definitely detrimental! Repeat the positive pattern!" – Andrie Wongso

Today, I am grateful for…

What is one negative thing you could easily eliminate from your life?

Day 21 __/__/__

"Hate. It has caused a lot of problems in this world
but has not solved one yet."
– Maya Angelou

Today, I am grateful for…

Does your home feel like a positive environment to you? Why or why not?

Day 22 __/__/__

"Having a positive mental attitude is asking how something can be done rather than saying it can't be done."
– Bo Bennett

Today, I am grateful for…

Who can you turn to when you need advice or support? How will that person help you?

Day 23 __/__/__

"Having the strength to tune out negativity and remain focused on what I want gives me the will and confidence to achieve my goals." – Gisele Bundchen

Today, I am grateful for…

What inspires you to be a better person? Why?

Day 24 __/__/__

"I always loved the spotlight, just not the negativity."
– Winnie Harlow

Today, I am grateful for…

What do you like to do to make yourself feel better when you're feeling down? Why?

Day 25 __/__/__

"I am thankful for all those who said no to me.
It's because of them I'm doing it myself."
– Albert Einstein

Today, I am grateful for…

When you're in a bad mood or feeling tired, do you prefer to be left alone or spend time with others? Why?

Day 26 __/__/__

"I am the greatest, I said that even before I knew I was."
– Muhammad Ali

Today, I am grateful for…

Make a list of positive "I am…" statements that you can read to yourself when you're feeling sad.

Day 27 __/__/__

"I been around negativity all my life.
To do something positive, it's a beautiful thing."
– Jay Rock

Today, I am grateful for…

What can you do today to make someone else's day a little better?

Day 28 __/__/__

"I don't feed into negativity. I thankfully don't. That's just me."
– Lil Yachty

Today, I am grateful for…

Do you find it easy to express your feelings? Why or why not?

Day 29 _/_/_

"I have no room in my life for any form of negativity
or nonacceptance."
– Ricky Williams

Today, I am grateful for…

It's only human to make mistakes! Write about a time when you could have used this reminder.

Day 30 __/__/__

"I may not have gone where I intended to go,
but I think I have ended up where I needed to be."
– Douglas Adams

Today, I am grateful for…

What are a few small things you could do to have a more positive attitude?

Day 31 __/__/__

"I prefer to celebrate every moment of my life
and not allow any negativity."
– Vivek Oberoi

Today, I am grateful for…

Who is the most positive person you know? How do you feel when you are around him or her?

Day 32 __/__/__

"I think you achieve a lot more through love than negativity."
– Alexa Chung

Today, I am grateful for…

Make a gratitude list of everything you're thankful for this week. Then, choose one thing to write about in detail.

Day 33 __/__/__

"I try to pace my life out and try not to be too involved with negativity and try to fix what I can fix in my life."
– Ghostface Killah

Today, I am grateful for…

Imagine your perfect day and write about what it would look like.

Day 34 __/__/__

"I will go as far as possible from people who like to complain because the negative energy is contagious."
– T Harv Eker

Today, I am grateful for…

Do you believe that setting a good intention for your day can help you have a better day? Why or why not?

Day 35 __/__/__

"I've had a lot of worries in my life,
most of which never happened."
– Mark Twain

Today, I am grateful for…

Create a morning mantra for yourself that you could use to start each day off right. Write about what it means to you.

Day 36 __/__/__

"If a person finds negative people in his life,
then he needs to mend his own nature than that of others,
for his own basic grounding decides the level of acidic or
toxicity surrounding him." – Anuj Somany

Today, I am grateful for…

What is something that always puts you in a good mood?

Day 37 __/__/__

"If my life does not last long then
why do negative quotations cover my beliefs?"
– Ahmad Fuadi

Today, I am grateful for…

Use your imagination. Write a description of yourself as seen through the eyes of someone who loves you and supports you emotionally. How do you feel after writing that description?

Day 38 __/__/__

"If someone tells you, "You can't" they really mean, "I can't."
– Sean Stephenson

Today, I am grateful for…

Focus on your strengths. Make a list of all your strengths and positive qualities.

Day 39 __/__/__

"If we always think negatively, the energy we will produce is not far from being pessimistic, not confident, upset, always complaining, and blaming others." – Rangga Umara

Today, I am grateful for…

What does it mean to you to have high self-esteem?

Day 40 __/__/__

"If we give something positive to others, it will return to us.
If we give negative, that negativity will be returned."
– Allu Arjun

Today, I am grateful for…

List 5 things you've done for others that made you feel good about yourself.

Day 41 __/__/__

"If you accept the expectations of others, especially negative ones, then you never will change the outcome."
– Michael Jordan

Today, I am grateful for…

BRAVE: What does this word mean to you? When have you been brave in the past?

Day 42 __/__/__

"If you dwell on your negativity you can never move on."
– Gina Miller

Today, I am grateful for…

Discuss one thing you can do right now that your future self will love you for later.

Day 43 __/__/__

"If you hear a voice within you say 'you cannot paint,' then by all means paint and that voice will be silenced."
— Vincent Van Gogh

Today, I am grateful for…

What unique traits do you have that your friends envy?

Day 44 __/__/__

"If you see it positively, the past is nothing bad.
There is only a beautiful past and valuable lessons."
– Mario Teguh

Today, I am grateful for…

Do you compare yourself to others? Discuss how this could be harmful to your self-esteem.

Day 45 __/__/__

"If you think positively,
you attract positive things into your life. Vice versa."
– Denny Santoso

Today, I am grateful for…

How could you make your life more positive?

Day 46 __/__/__

"If you want light to come into your life,
you need to stand where it is shining."
– Guy Finley

Today, I am grateful for…

Create a playlist of mood-boosting songs and why you enjoy listening to each when you need a lift.

Day 47 __/__/__

"I'm here to clean minds of negativity
and build confidence in others."
– Mod Sun

Today, I am grateful for…

Discuss your support system for times you are feeling down on yourself. How do they help boost your confidence?

Day 48 __/__/__

"I'm the kind of person who doesn't really focus
on more negativity. I'm a positive person,
and I look at things in a positive way." – Caster Semenya

Today, I am grateful for…

What is your favorite inspirational quote? How does it help you?

Day 49 __/__/__

"In every disaster that befell you, remember to look in the mirror and ask about what power you can try to draw positive lessons from that incident." – Epictetus

Today, I am grateful for…

Write about something you need to tell someone who is negatively affecting your life.

Day 50 __/__/__

"Instead of worrying about what you cannot control,
divert your energy to what you can create."
– Roy T. Bennet

Today, I am grateful for…

List 10 things you are thankful for in your life right now. Don't forget to focus on yourself - qualities, body parts, skills, etc.

Day 51 __/__/__

"It does not matter how slowly you go
as long as you do not stop."
– Confucius

Today, I am grateful for…

Who inspires you now? Write a letter to that person.

Day 52 __/__/__

"It is never too late to be what you might have been."
– George Eliot

Today, I am grateful for…

Discuss something you want to learn, improve, or change that would make you feel better about yourself. Create an action plan to get this taken care of.

Day 53 __/__/__

"It's better to be an optimist who is sometimes wrong
than a pessimist who is always right."
– Unknown

Today, I am grateful for…

Pen a thank you letter to your mind and/or body.

Day 54 __/__/__

"It's difficult to look on the bright side when you're surrounded by negativity."
– Amy Morin

Today, I am grateful for…

Write about past fear you were able to overcome. How did you feel before and after the experience?

Day 55 __/__/__

"I've learned to laugh most of the negativity off."
– Tomi Lahren

Today, I am grateful for…

COURAGE: What does this word mean to you? How have you shown courage recently?

Day 56 __/__/__

"Letting go of negative people doesn't mean you hate them. It just means that you love yourself."
– Anonymous

Today, I am grateful for…

What is the most negative thought in your brain right now? Discuss how you can eliminate it from your mind.

Day 57 __/__/__

"Life is for life, not thinking. In order to live freely, we must free ourselves from negative thoughts."
– Vernon Howard

Today, I am grateful for…

Discuss your best personality trait. How do your friends describe you? What do they love about you?

Day 58 __/__/__

"Life is not about how much trouble comes to us, but about how positively we are able to respond to all these problems."
– Bambang Pamungkas

Today, I am grateful for…

Talk about your favorite role model as if you are described him/her to a friend that does not know this person. What about this person makes you look up to him/her?

Day 59 __/__/__

"Love yourself. It is essential to stay positive because beauty comes from the inside out."
– Jenn Proske

Today, I am grateful for…

Devise a plan for each of your three priority goals. How do you plan to make the dreams a reality?

Day 60 __/__/__

"Making mistakes is the right of active people. Ordinary people are always negative, who spend their time proving that they are not wrong." – Ingvar Kamprad

Today, I am grateful for…

Create a list of goals you plan to accomplish in the next year. Choose your three priority goals that you plan to focus on most.

Day 61 __/__/__

"Minds are like flowers, they only open when the time is right."
– Stephen Richards

Today, I am grateful for…

CONFIDENCE: Write what this word means to you. How can improve your confidence?

Day 62 __/__/__

"Negative people can only infest you with discouragements when they find you around… Just get lost and get saved!"
– Israelmore Ayivor

Today, I am grateful for…

Think about a time when you regretted your decision. Write out how you felt and create a written apology for yourself.

Day 63 __/__/__

"Negative thinking is proportional to the value of the creator, and the results of the implementation."
– Ansel Adams

Today, I am grateful for…

Discuss 3 reasons why you deserve to be loved.

Day 64 __/__/__

"Negativity is cannibalistic. The more you feed it,
the bigger and stronger it grows."
– Bobby Darnel

Today, I am grateful for…

Describe a mistake you made in the last week. How can you prevent the same mistake again?

Day 65 __/__/__

"Negativity is the enemy of creativity."
– David Lynch

Today, I am grateful for…

Name 5 things you did right today, no matter how small or seemingly insignificant.

Day 66 __/__/__

"Negativity may knock at your door,
but that doesn't mean you have to let it in."
– Anonymous

Today, I am grateful for…

Write about a time you were recognized for your accomplishments at work or school.

Day 67 __/__/__

"No matter how valuable you are and your ideas, fools will certainly play both of you down, so exclude yourselves from the inflammatory environs of fools." – Michael Bassey Johnson

Today, I am grateful for…

Write about the most recent time you were really happy.

Day 68 _/_/_

"No matter the amount of negativity you're presented with, five minutes from now could be your best moment."
– Mod Sun

Today, I am grateful for…

Write down your best coping mechanisms and how they've helped you

Day 69 __/__/__

"Nobody can make you feel inferior without your consent."
–Eleanor Roosevelt

Today, I am grateful for…

Create yourself a positive affirmation.

Day 70 __/__/__

""""Optimists have a habit of explaining anything that happens to them positively. Pessimists explain anything that happens to them negatively." – Haryanto Kandani

Today, I am grateful for…

List all the things that will happen and come into your life if you never stop dreaming.

Day 71 __/__/__

"Our greatest weakness lies in giving up. The most certain way to succeed is always to try just one more time."
– Thomas Edison

Today, I am grateful for…

What makes you feel good about yourself?

Day 72 __/__/__

"People who project negativity typically have low self-esteem. They feel badly about themselves, and their negativity is simply a reflection of those feelings." – Hendrie Weisinger

Today, I am grateful for…

What do you want more of in your life?

Day 73 __/__/__

"Positive things happen to people who are positive."
– Sarah Beeny

Today, I am grateful for…

How would your best friend describe you?

Day 74 __/__/__

"Positive thinking will let you do everything better than negative thinking will."
– Zig Ziglar

Today, I am grateful for…

What are you grateful for about your personality?

Day 75 __/__/__

"Remember…Whoever is trying to bring you down
is already below you."
– Ziad K. Abdelnour

Today, I am grateful for…

What brings you peace and why?

Day 76 __/__/__

"Run away from people who are negative."
– Greg S. Reid

Today, I am grateful for…

Write about a time where you felt extremely proud of yourself.

Day 77 __/__/__

"Sensitive souls draw in the negativity of others
because they are so open."
– John Gray

Today, I am grateful for…

List the things you like about the way you look.

Day 78 __/__/__

"Some people can't function without negativity because bringing down others makes them feel better."
– Anonymous

Today, I am grateful for…

What's the bravest thing you've ever done?

Day 79 __/__/__

"Staying positive does not mean that things will turn out okay.
Rather it is knowing that you will be okay
no matter how things turn out." – Unknown

Today, I am grateful for…

Write down a time that you were convinced you couldn't do something but then achieved it? How did it feel?

Day 80 __/__/__

"Stop allowing other people to dilute
or poison your day with their words or opinions."
– Steve Maraboli

Today, I am grateful for…

Who am I without my negative thoughts?

Day 81 __/__/__

"Take chances, make mistakes. That's how you grow. Pain nourishes your courage. You have to fail in order to practice being brave." – Mary Tyler Moore

Today, I am grateful for…

What triggers my negative thoughts? How do you plan to overcome them?

Day 82 __/__/__

"That's my gift. I let that negativity roll off me like water off a duck's back. If it's not positive, I didn't hear it. If you can overcome that, fights are easy." – George Foreman

Today, I am grateful for…

Where do my negative thoughts come from? How do you plan to manage them?

Day 83 __/__/__

"The ability to be patient and survive in a positive mind
is the basis of further human leaps."
– Merry Triana

Today, I am grateful for…

Who do you need to spend more time with? What are your plans?

Day 84 __/__/__

"The best way to gain self-confidence
is to do what you are afraid to do."
– Unknown

Today, I am grateful for…

Describe a priceless moment you had.

Day 85 __/__/__

"The difference between stumbling blocks
and stepping stones is how you use them."
– Unknown

Today, I am grateful for…

What's the next best step forward from here?

Day 86 _/_/_

"The first thing I built inside of me to be able to face the day with enthusiasm was to create as many positive thoughts as possible." – Merry Triana

Today, I am grateful for…

If you learn from your mistakes, why are you always so afraid to make a mistake?

Day 87 __/__/__

"The greatest discovery of all time is that a person can change his future by merely changing his attitude."
– Oprah Winfrey

Today, I am grateful for…

What excuses do you need to stop making?

Day 88 __/__/__

"The human self must subjugate self-war against the negative."
– Pepeng Soebardi Ferrasta

Today, I am grateful for…

What gets you excited about life?

Day 89 __/__/__

"The more you dwell on what you don't have,
the more you get what you don't want."
– Unknown

Today, I am grateful for…

What activities help you feel most like yourself?

Day 90 __/__/__

"The more you feed your mind with positive thoughts,
the more you can draw great things into your life."
– Roy T. Bennet

Today, I am grateful for…

What would you do differently if you knew nobody would judge you?

Day 91 __/__/__

"The most common way people give up their power
is by thinking they don't have any."
– Alice Walker

Today, I am grateful for…

Write about a time you thought about the worst-case scenario and it turned out completely fine.

Day 92 __/__/__

"The next time you feel slightly uncomfortable with the pressure in your life, remember no pressure, no diamonds. Pressure is a part of success." – Eric Thomas

Today, I am grateful for…

One way I could love myself more is...

Day 93 __/__/__

"The only place where your dream becomes impossible is in your own thinking."
– Robert H Schuller

Today, I am grateful for…

What do you know you're great at?

Day 94 __/__/__

"The past has no power over the present moment."
– Eckhart Tolle

Today, I am grateful for…

Who, or what, needs your forgiveness?

Day 95 __/__/__

"The person who says it cannot be done
should not interrupt the person who is doing it."
– Chinese Proverb

Today, I am grateful for…

What are you holding on to that you need to let go of?

Day 96 __/__/__

"There are so many great things in life;
why dwell on negativity?"
– Zendaya

Today, I am grateful for…

What's one problem you're thankful you don't have?

Day 97 __/__/__

"There is little difference in people, but that little difference makes a big difference. The little difference is attitude. The big difference is whether it is positive or negative."
– W. Clement Stone

Today, I am grateful for…

What do you do to combat negativity and reassure yourself of how amazing you are?

Day 98 _/_/_

"Think positively, no matter how hard your life is."
– Ali bin Abi Talib

Today, I am grateful for…

Write down three words that describe how you feel right now- then write down the antonyms of each of those words and think about times you've felt those feelings.

Day 99 __/__/__

"Try to create inner peace with yourself; try to understand, forgive, and forget. Replace with positive thoughts. Life is change. Change for the better." – Andrie Wongso

Today, I am grateful for…

Why do you deserve to be happy?

Day 100 __/__/__

"Turn on your life to the full and focus on the positive things."
– Matt Cameron

Today, I am grateful for…

Write a love letter to yourself.

"We are all here for some special reason.
Stop being a prisoner of your past.
Become the architect of your future."
– Robin Sharma

CPSIA information can be obtained
at www.ICGtesting.com
Printed in the USA
BVHW030037170720
583815BV00004BA/782